Wild Fire

POETIC PRISMS

6/4/19

For Karen & Tim —
Let your wild fire rage!
w/ Love,
CJ Sherry

SHERRY SADOFF HANCK

BALBOA.
PRESS

A DIVISION OF HAY HOUSE

Balboa Press books may be ordered through booksellers or by contacting:

Balboa Press
A Division of Hay House
1663 Liberty Drive
Bloomington, IN 47403
www.balboapress.com
1 (877) 407-4847

Because of the dynamic nature of the Internet, any web addresses or
links contained in this book may have changed since publication and
may no longer be valid. The views expressed in this work are solely those
of the author and do not necessarily reflect the views of the publisher,
and the publisher hereby disclaims any responsibility for them.

The author of this book does not dispense medical advice or prescribe the use
of any technique as a form of treatment for physical, emotional, or medical
problems without the advice of a physician, either directly or indirectly. The
intent of the author is only to offer information of a general nature to help you
in your quest for emotional and spiritual well-being. In the event you use any
of the information in this book for yourself, which is your constitutional right,
the author and the publisher assume no responsibility for your actions.

Cover Image by Colleen Attara

Print information available on the last page.

ISBN: 978-1-5043-6579-6 (sc)
ISBN: 978-1-5043-6580-2 (e)

Balboa Press rev. date: 11/22/2016

Contents

LIGHT

WILD FLOWERS ~ NATURE'S WINDOW

Dedication

Dedicated to family and friends, strangers and neighbors and all curious sentient beings.

May we connect through the deepest expressions of our hearts and continue to climb the mountains of our dreams, supporting each other the whole way up.

Acknowledgements

I would be lost in the ether without the grounding force of my family, friends & teachers.

My husband Brian, whose love transformed my life and brought it all into focus. You gave me the greatest gifts, our children, and continue to lift me up with your generosity, compassion and love. Happy New Day, every day!

Our children ~ Cassidy Sky, Jasmine Rain & Bailey Dawn, each a unique gift that I get to unwrap a little every day. You are the source of my abiding breath and beating heart. I am humbled by the vastness of this love.

My parents ~ Robert & Joan Sadoff who amaze and inspire me with every uttered word and action taken. Your courage, compassion, wisdom and love are the foliage of my forest. You planted the garden in which I now get to dance and play. I am eternally grateful.

My siblings & their spouses ~ Debbie & Ritchie, David & Claudia, Julie & Malek, each of whom create landscapes rich in color, line and dimension. My life is enriched by your presence and the heart-felt architecture you inspire.

My nieces and nephews ~ Jessie, Eric, Haley, Rachel, Jake, Azad and Maya. It is a privilege to watch each of you grow into the stunning people you continue to become. Each, for your unique voice and heart, have made my heart explode with love.

Liz Conner & Tom Carroll, whose family-owned businesses thrive from their beautiful hearts ~ I am forever grateful to be part of the Prancing Peacock & Crossing Vineyards families!

Cyndi Lee, whose first OM Yoga Studio on 14th Street in NYC provided me with the roots of my practice and first-love feeling for yoga (from which so much of my path was revealed).

Theresa Macy & Karin Eisen, my anatomy gurus, for offering me a whole new vocabulary (of the body) from which to be inspired... stay tuned!

Rabbi Anna Boswell-Levy for inviting me deeper into the contemplative process and showing me different ways to practice.

Colleen Attara, storyteller...eco-artist...treasure hunter, for showing up every time I ask you to share your talents, gifts and enormous heart! In this case, for wrapping this collection in your art by designing the cover.

My friends, too numerous to list, you own a huge chunk of real estate in my heart! You each add spice to this life and make every moment an adventure.

Gratitude meets fortune at the crossroads of love.

Introduction

Writing is one way I choose to expose what dwells in my heart.

Words are like ingredients, sweet and savory, bitter, tangy or spicy, they combine to create tasty bites and fill our senses. Words are like stones or bricks on which we can build structures to deepen understanding, prod curiosity, encourage thought and promote play. Words can be simple or complicated, frilly or plain; they can hurt or heal, demote or exalt, excite or soothe.

Because we are complicated beings who experience a huge range of emotions and experiences, having access to a wide vocabulary is helpful when looking to express oneself with precision.

I have found that poetry is more permissive in its form, providing the chef or builder of these word structures a wider range of creative license. I have also noticed a proclivity toward certain words over others at different times in my life.

This collection is a departure, in some ways, from the love-centric nature of my last collection, *Love's Wild Journey ~ Poems from an Untamed Heart*. It explores how shadow, light and nature form the seed of love but can often reveal deeper truths.

We live in the gray space between black and white and are often called upon to dance within the lick of flames generated by our words, thoughts and actions. Our breath fans the flames so that we may reach beyond our pre-determined heights and move in harmony within the world we live.

May your wild fire push the shadows closer to their edge so that you may dance more fully in the light!

I wish you all eternal love!

Love & Peace from the Path,
Sherry

It only takes
One person
To believe in you
For amazing things
To happen.
What if that person
Was you?

SHADOWS

W

Wrapped in a cloak of heaviness
Warmed by thoughts of sleep
Wondering how I got here
Wishing thoughts were not so deep

Shadow Takes the Lead

I followed my shadow home
dancing in my new pink shoes
allowing them to take the lead

Cradling a heavy heart
pierced by life
excitement strangely surfaces

My feet move effortlessly
shrinking the shadowy shapes
brightening the world and
lightening my steps

Barely feeling the ground
my soles support my journey
my soul sees the pink canvas and
smiles

Alchemy

It is alchemy that moves me from the
darkness of total misunderstanding into the
light of wakeful knowing ~
It turns the base metal of mental agony into
golden rays of courage and possibility ~
I move my body and mind with my breath
linking the academic to the visceral
working to feel this process and its nuances ~
Ancient and active, I am caught in the surge
of this flowing transformation ~
Life's brevity is the great equalizer
Sentience is my doorway into the laboratory
Detachment is the key that opens the door

Angels & Demons

The demon drops heavy
in the pit of my gut
wrenching the soft tissues
transforming the calm sweetness
emblematic of my being
into something other
    Irrational
    Dark
    Seething

I bow to the presence
acknowledging its truth
then dip my heart to hold it
    Tenderly
    Curiously
    Lovingly

What surfaces is quite complex
it exists without definition or form
an energy current that carries
with it every experience, feeling and
thought that ever crossed
my winding, crooked path

For now, the dormant demon sinks back
beneath the still surface waters
creating gentle rapids that keep
things flowing, moving

I do not banish these little devils
They are essential
I honor their wisdom
keeping pace with what
arises in their wake

Pulling back from the edge of ego
I laugh from that deep cavernous pit
remembering all that gave birth to
what seems demonic
and laugh louder

Are those angel wings I see?

Blank

Blank paper
Blank mind
Searching for something
I cannot find

Does it matter?
Do you care?
If I am here
Or I am there?

See

I need you
   your presence unsettles me

I need you to see
   that which disturbs you through my eyes

I need you so I can see
   the dark spaces and blind spots that keep me from
fully inhabiting my
truest self

Season Song

Songs have often themed around
life and its seasons
Joni's went "round and round"
While Terry Jacks crooned about
"Seasons in the Sun"
We cry, laugh and ponder
as we listen to the lyrics
that often tell us part of our
own story.

Time seems to crawl when we are
young and eager to celebrate our next birthday
We grow into and around ourselves
moving away and returning with gifts
many of which wait to be unwrapped
until we reach the next sign, detour or
bump in the road.

The seasons change
People move away
Get married
Have children
Careers
Travel
Change careers
Divorce
Hide
Dance
Rejoice
Die

Throughout it all
Mother Nature does her dance
Winter turns to Spring
Spring to Summer
Summer to Fall

Though time moves more quickly
at different stages of our lives
Still, we listen to the music

The Sound of Ego

what is that sound?
the one that
rattles me
from my
perfectly constructed
peaceful
place

closer inspection
reveals it is the
rapid
pulse
of my heart
beating

practice
makes perfect
so I
breathe
slowing the
unhealthy spread
of ego
in its tracks

this work requires
the witness
to awaken

curious
I close my eyes
the view is clear
but the path
must be tidied

there is much
work to be
done and
untold miles to
tread

no rakes or
shovels will
make free the way
so with an
open mind
I sit and
breathe
abiding in the
abundance
of my own
humanness

Bourbon

I take a sip
It goes down smooth
radiating a trail
like embers
warming my throat and
waking me up

The ice melts
diluting the potent, rich
flavors
the heat all but vanishes
fingers feel the cool
damp glass
I gulp rather than sip
inviting the final drops
to find their way
the ring of water on the table
glistens in the dim lamp light

I use my bare hand to wipe it
dry

Why?

At fourteen years of age
existential questions
loomed larger than my years
seeming separate
other
amusing
in a way that
insulated me from
curiosity and context
which might reveal
kernels of truth

The college years
presented a new
perspective
as the lens
through which
life was viewed
expanded
including worlds
previously hidden
from the sheltered
universe of my
formative years

The twenties
single
working
playing
among the urban landscape
offered the questions up

like a pu pu platter
of ideas
to chew on
and take home in
portioned containers
for later

As marriage
and children entered
the realm,
my thirties
both embodied
and ignored
the questions
of existence
as attention and focus
lived in the
urgency
of now
and had a clarity
unique
to that time

Now,
well into my forties,
the questions
I have pondered
most of my life
have a tangible
quality
one informed
as much by
death and disease
as by miracles,

love
and unexpected
joy

Lying still,
Like a corpse
I breathe into
The container that is
my body
while I release
thoughts
expectations
judgments
I am acutely aware
of the
life-force
coursing through
the pathways of
my physical self
Being
Breathing
Becoming

The questions,
my old friends,
return periodically
I surrender to their query
curious and awake.

Why?

Markers of Time

My hands
they are
changing
but I still
recognize them
as my
own

Though they
hold
a different
form
from the
fingers
of my youth
the skin
still snuggles
to blood and bone
with soft elasticity
expressing the time
between then
and now

Once strong
smooth and
expressive
visceral seekers
of experience
feeling everything
they touched with
curiosity and a sense of
adventure

Resilient
their new
wisdom tangible
blue veins pulsating
softly calloused from use
express strength
healing
magic
with a
light touch

Some day
perhaps
not long away
I will see
my hands
not as
my own
but of those
belonging to
my future
self
greet them proudly
from this place
and wave
hello

Container

I am nothing like you
We are the same
Who are you?
I am.
I am a unique expression of love
My vessel carries a measure of fear
But I will not be guided by any
Ration of alarm
I am.

Aperture of Light

Through the tiny pinhole
In the massive gray
I see a point of luminosity
Obscured by the thrashing rain and
Cloud of confusion
It struggles to be seen

Squinting, the tiny dot expands
Taking me into its warmth and light

Questioning "I" dentity

Who would
I be
if I had a different
name
eye color
or shape?
Can a heart
differentiate
between
tall and short
beige and brown
a smile, a frown?

How am I
informed
by external
input?
Wild curls and
Ample ass
Clear voice
Perception's lens

Is my
purpose
attached to
my idea of
who I think I am
or
is my sense of self
defined by my
mission?

If I deconstruct
myself from
the outside-in
what will I find?
Self, Other or
All?
Is there even an
I
to ask?

The Infinite

What has no container
takes shape in
the ever-expanding
Heart of Love

The sky is infinite
yet it holds color
and the collective memory
of sunsets, sunrises
and all shades of blue
It also takes on form
when clouds,
white, gray or stormy
dot its landscape
allowing us a glimpse
of its unending
Universal
story

The body
carries something infinite
within its walls
Skin wraps muscle & bone
giving us form
Blood and breath
give us a life
rich with boundless
possibilities

When the vessel that works to
contain this energy
understands it finite-ness
it is set free

My Teacher

the uncomfortable moment
that guides me to clarity
and reminds me to breathe

the moment before I raise my voice
running into the frustration
and the stillness of the quiet
that follows

the irrational feeling I get
when my buttons are pushed
and I react without thinking
humbled

my teachers
fear, pride
jealousy, greed
insecurity, doubt
Love
Gratitude
Breath

Life.

Pan's Shadow

Peter Pan
the boy who didn't want
to grow up,
was compelled to
leave Never Land
to retrieve his
shadow

why?

did he just want
to see Wendy?
or was he moved
by a deeper,
more powerful force?
could he have defeated the
dominant shadow of
Captain Hook without
embracing his own
darkness?

the window
portal of light
and lightlessness
passage
to a world of
growth and
change
with promises of
flight to the unknown
one that leaves

childhood dreams
in the nursery
on the path to
maturity
beckons us all

this threshold
a thin boundary
between deep sleep and
being fully awake
offers both
pause and choice
each and every day
draw the shade
against the world
or open it wide
inviting in the bright light and
embracing the shadows it casts

Start Where You Are

We start where we are
And meet ourselves there
Following the cosmic arrows that
Point us this way and that
Moving with determination for a while then
Pulsating to a meandering gait

We wander and wonder
Break earth beneath our feet!
Wade, float, swim on the waters!
Soar through the air of dreams!
One breath yields to the next until
They overlap, blurring distinction

So it is with a purpose-driven life when
One path of action seamlessly unfolds into
Another into
Another into
Another ...
Nothing is separate
Mission and heart are in line
Pushing us to keep exploring
Landing where we are and continuing to
Meet our selves there

Chew Slowly

I like to dabble
    Feast on small portions
Fully embody life's most
    Perfect distortions
They're sacred and flawed
    Precious and true
So I take a big bite
    And relax as I chew

Waking Up

Fatigue threatens to
blur clarity
Eyelids are heavy with the
weight of truth
I step gingerly off the
rapidly moving path
To rest, to surrender
To be

The view is a convergence of
all things
As active witness
I am in awe
all there for the taking
I pause,
feeling the absorption as it
seeps into my skin
Clearing the way to once again
Wake up

Home

Footsteps, shadows and whispers
Imprints of the living
Outlines of inner workings
Quiet reminders to be aware

Stomping in the bright light with loud voices
Opens a tiny door to enchantment
Where subtlety reigns and guides
Energy flows unencumbered, free
Sacred and profane dissolve into the ether

Soft footsteps show the way
Cloak of shadow provides refuge
Whispered vibrations point to truth
Welcome home

To Be or Not

"To be or not to be"
Is that really the question?
Is it root, stem or
Leafy distraction?

To love or not to love?
To fear or not to fear?
To take the risk or
Choose not to hear?

There are many questions in
Life to ponder
Sitting still so mind
Won't wander and
May lead gently to
Something fonder

I bow to Shakespeare and
His poetic musing
And honor his words with
No excusing

To end this rhyme I ask you this
Is it to Woe or live in Bliss?

Compass

Don't despair
When all seems bleak
Permanence is an illusion
As good times fade, so do bad
As if they're in collusion

Dance with me to the beat
Of life's ongoing pulsation
Our hearts beat together
Bright and gray weather
Docking in one station

You're my North Star
When I am lost
Your twinkle guides my way
I'm grateful for our beautiful life
And look forward to each new day!

Free

when words fail
default to feeling
sit on ground
when mind is reeling
movement stills
afflictions flee
charge on forward
you are free

Resting in Shadow

In the quiet darkness things arise
    often distorted, like a shadow
Heartbeat soars, fear unleashed
    the slightest sadness felt as sorrow

The dawn brings light to shine upon
    the demons in their nest
From this fresh view they've all but vanished
    heart and mind are now at rest

Heart's Home

Walking through my halls and rooms
it is clear to me that it is
the ongoing gathering of souls and stories
that build a home

The mug on the ledge given to me by a beloved teacher
The desk that once belonged to my mother
Numerous art pieces crafted by dear friends
who've passed through my life and keep me winking at
my edge

Every item has a story and a lingering feeling
And then we build lodgings to contain the chronicles

But can a home ever wall out the current of
connection that must keep rolling?
Additions and deletions cycle through
Our nomadic journeys
while the essence of home rests fully
in one's heart

Stories from the Mist

The mist descends like a veil
expanding with a steady pulse
forever changing the rhythm and view

Through this lens the scenes
unfold to tell a bigger story
one which offers untethered possibility
grounded in the spaces between
imagination and formulation
reality and perception
confusion and clarity
fear and love

The subtleties of motion
lie somewhere inside the stillness
imperceptibly rocking and lolling
the mind and heart to a place
of calm

As the dew from the mist
settles on the skin's surface
something deeper is revealed

The pictures fade into feeling
afflictions dissolve into wisdom
The End is The Beginning

Distortion

It is a distorted
shape of who
I think I am
and follows me
wherever
I go
Nipping at
my heels
with relentless
urgency

Sometimes screaming
for my attention
and other times
quietly lurking
safely tucked in
the rays of the sun

Light reveals
and dissolves
its form
but it is always
there

My shadow
a silo of memory
inviting courage
to face demons
big and small
It is a reminder
that without
darkness
there is no
light at all

Shimmer

Something shimmers
in that dark space
like gazing into
a pool of water at night
under a bright moon
ripples of energy
move out from center
encompassing a world
within a world
within a world

hints of form
create a nebulous
structure through which
I operate; stretching ever
toward the light
bathing in the glow
of possibility

working hard not to
judge that always-changing
space; breathing deeply to
test the limits of its lines
and my ability to direct
the way

grateful for the chance
to cool off in the shadows
after dancing all day
in the sun

Finding Flow

Resting
In the mystery
Struggling
To un-know
Surrendering
To Spirit
Finding
The flow

Old habits
Rise
New ones
Form
Which ones to
Honor
Which ones to
Mourn

Dissolving the
Lines
That divide and
Define
Like a baby
Discovers
What to
Refine

So it goes and
It goes
Around and
Around
Left in its
Wake
Is the
Primordial
Sound

Conception

Burning through
the fog
clarity is forming
like an embryo of
ideas

encapsulated
in the warmth
and safety
in the womb of
imagination

sown
in the heart and
tilled by life, its
challenges and
triumphs

crafted by
unseen forces
joined in the daily
ordinary miracles of each
moment

I revel in the
complexity
of its form
reflected in nature's simple
wisdom

confusion contains this
seed of clarity;
patience and practice
reveal its essence and
mystery

Blow Your Mind

Imagine
no beginning
and
no end

Time
as we measure it
an illusion

Wrap your mind
around
the enormity

Hone in on
the moment
surrender
to the abyss

close eyes
take a deep breath
sigh it out
into the ether
of all things

Pinpoint
the twinkle of light
that anchors
consciousness
to something
beyond thought

Hearts beating
around the world
become a unified
drumbeat
connecting us all
within the existence of
beginning-less time

Waiting Room

The same blade that
forged the
words
framed and held the
silence

Once removed from
The safety of its
scabbard
its incisive message
cut into the
fragile space between
Intellect and feeling
consciousness and habit
fear and surrender

The ones in white
sliced through my
complacent mind
And led me to a room
Pristine
Institutional
Sterile
Quiet

Empty but for my thoughts
The corrosive silence
Like rust on metal
Ate through me
Bit by bit

Somewhere in the
silent din and
dark corners dusted with
my rusty remains
I am
Given a chance to
Fight back

Excavating Fear

How do I reach the fear that
Lives deep inside my fibers
And what do I do with it
When I find it?

Edge of Light

Hope is the light at the
Edge of darkness

Impermanent, it rides the
Same breeze that
Moves through the trees and
The sky ~ the same wind that
Blows through our bodies
Transforming us from
Day to day

Attaching to hope is like
Trying to contain the clouds
To preserve a memory and
Hold it as truth

Release the grip and watch as the
Terrain shifts, changing our
Inner landscapes with every
Sacred breath

Sound of Silence

there is
movement in

stillness as
there is
sound in

silence

the space
between breaths
is a
choice
made

over and
over
day by
day
moment to
moment

in that
space
is all
that
*matter*s

The Call

Breathe on purpose
Inhale the world
All that's possible
Will be unfurled

Rest in wonder
Hold head high
Make some effort
Exhale and sigh

I hear the call
From someplace deep
Rousing my body
To wake from sleep

The mind comes next
And then my heart
It will take a whole lifetime
To the decipher this art

What it's saying
Cannot be heard
It must be lived
Without a word

Fruits of the Earth

I bow deeply
Connecting
Offering my judgments and
Moments of self-righteousness
To the earth for
Transmutation
Purification
I bow deeper
Rooting
Planting my generosity and
Goodness for the benefit
Of others
Awaiting the first fruit
So I can give it away

The Key

Her light flickers dimly as
Sadness drapes her frail frame

Loss and desperation shade her small world
The lines drawn to contain her were
Colored by someone else
Something other

Imagination, passion and possibility are
Faint fumes
From another lifetime

Softly, I direct her to the key she
Wears around her neck
The one that opens the dusty
Cobweb-ridden suitcase
That contains her greatness

I remind her simply that she need only
Unpack it to reveal this forgotten truth

And that she, and she alone
Holds the key

Foot Notes

My body is a map of where I've traveled
    on the earth and in my heart
My feet hold stories of many sacred steps
    softly trod on soil, sand and stone
In the stillness, imagination simmers
    stimulating thoughts and memories
    marinating in my mind awaiting the
    heart's permission to surface
My muscles are messengers of truth
    holding in their fibers that which my
    senses would choose to ignore ~ they
    filter toxic energy of negativity, fear, regret
    often manifesting in physical pain or discomfort
I do not always know what they are trying to tell me
    but I do my best to listen
Within my bones is a deeper understanding
    they hold the intuitive part that just knows
    giving form to function and movement to mystery
My body is a storybook, writing my memoir in
    every moment, with every breath
Much as I try to edit, the narrative will not allow it
    forcing the unabridged version into the world
In moments of clarity, I walk with reverence
    feeling the power of each step and
    whisper possible plots into the wind

Trapped

I see the trap and run right for it
Thoughtless of the outcome
Driven by something primal
Dangling bait lures me in
Enticing my curious instinct
Oblivious of the feeling
Sure to follow

Danger & Do Not Enter signs
Yellow caution tape
Locked doors
Red velvet ropes
All designed to keep people out
Do not slow me down

"Don't take the bait"
He tells me
Much too late to
Make a difference

I gobble it up

Trapped by my habits
Trapped in my mind
Trapped for now

The sign ahead reads
Welcome
I see it clearly
All that was locked in
Is now free

The Village

The space
Empty of meaning
Ripe with potential
Quickly filled with love

A gathering of
Strangers with smiles
Threaded together as one
Beautiful cloth of curiosity

Colors of every hue
rode the breath
Of our beautiful teacher
Laughter echoed as
Spirits melded

Unity painted the walls
Wisdom bounced from
One precious heart to
The next

"SHIT!"

The sound pierced our
Bubble of peace
Heads turned as
Gasps escaped
Mouths agape with
Surprise and fear

One of our brothers
Had fallen

The intimacy so sudden
The reality of impermanence
Close enough to taste
Reaction was quick and compassionate
Tendrils of love
Palpable and singly directed
Revealed the instinct of
Basic goodness in all who were
Present

To this village, I bow

Question

When you close your
Eyes
Are you going in
Or closing
Out?
When you move into the
World
Do you act from
Love
Or doubt?
Replace judgment with
Compassion
There's a time to
Whisper
And a time to
Shout!

Ownership

Own your shit

Thoughts
Dark, bleak
Wise, funny

Feelings
Blue, mad
Sparkling, sunny

Words
Hurtful, helpful
Thoughtful, punny

Actions
Harsh, subtle
On the money

Breath
Shallow, smooth
Sweet like honey

Give everything else away

Start Here

if you're a being of light
you will cast a shadow
to explore the great depths
you must start where it's shallow

Alone

Surrounded by people
Meaningful exchanges punctuate the
Spaces that bridge the gap created by
Silence
Friends sprout up everywhere
Like a field covered with daisies
Where do I run first?
Which flower distinguishes itself as
True?
Perennials blossom cyclically in the
Garden of dreams
This soil of awake-ness only
Produces annuals which
Require attention and nurturing
To grow

Which ones will grow to the sun with me
Share its rays and
Thrive when the sun turns to wind & rain
I am alone with each blade of grass as I
Contemplate the fickle nature of
Weather
Flowers
Friends
Not separate from my mind
My heart feels
Sad
Full
Heavy
Surrounded by so many yet
I am still alone

Humble Warrior

humbling moments
are gifts for the soul
reminding us to be present
and grateful and whole

Unlimited Do-Overs

somewhere between
here and there
ideas get shattered
should i care?
in the space between
now and then
they get rebuilt
i start again

Wake Up!

wake up! wake up!
he implored us all
wake up! wake up!
do not miss life's call

Rabbit Hole

when plunging down
the rabbit hole
take a moment to
look around

it may not be
that you are falling
rather looking
to be found

Diving Deep

It's heavy
Weighted down by
Grief
Loss
Judgment
Misunderstanding

Energetically paralyzed
I seek to escape
Moving deeper
With my mind
My heart follows

Sadness peeks through the
Veil of being to
Pursue the soft spots
To poke them
Shuck them like an
Oyster whose pearl
Got lost

Deep in the dark waters
I search for a hint
Of light to
Guide me back to
The surface where I
Can float
Buoyant
Weightless
Free

Beyond Words

Complicated by
Words
I fail to purify
This demon
Which intends to
Do me harm

It will take a
Spiritual army
To slay this
Ill-willed entity

As leader of this
Combat team, I nod
Knowingly
Toward my heart
And watch the
Creature of my custom
Evaporate in a flurry of
Unformed words

Just. Be.

pondering the moment
curious and fresh
bid farewell today
then and now enmesh

in the stillness
lives the truth
and the many mysteries
the breath can sleuth

look ahead with wonder
look back and smile
look around, there you are
just BE a while

Pit

Down
Down
Down
Deep down
Beneath the layers of
Being and breath
Is a pit
Planted at creation
Rooted to the core
Its hard shell
Impermeable to light
Impervious to circumstance
It cradles my
Deepest fear

Hard Truths Told

trembling
eyes blur
mind leaves body
to do
what must
be done

truth
wraps around
the space
created by
itself

there is
no other
way

weaving
a story
to confound
the essential
truth
is not
an option

fear
falls away
revealing a
larger
reality

integrity
surfaces

calm
and serenity
replace
trembling hands

truth
heals cracks
and makes
whole

Stars in Your Eyes

Stars fill your eyes with light
Giving you the strength to see beyond the surface
What lies beneath the shallow topsoil are
Microscopic ecosystems designed to magnify
    Beauty
Naked to the eye
Obvious to the heart
Abundant in the natural world
    Vision goes beyond simple sight
    Feeling for the splendor in a teardrop
Magnificence in a tree
Sweetness cradled in the heart of sadness
    Beauty is not fragile or conditional
    It is the lens

Sad

The sadness is so
profound
It prevents me from any
rational thought

It obscures my vision
Chokes my throat
Lays waste to
my heart

Ghostly Grasp

deep inside
the whisper is an
echo an
echo
hinting at
something of an
ancient scream
haunting the halls of
memory

Here
Here
It seems to
Call out with a
Ghostly growl
Beckoning to
Wake up

It never goes away
Completely
That piece from
Youth
Tender & soft yet
Unrelenting

Its grasp
Grips my heart
Firmly held it
Softens the
Callouses that have
Formed around it

In the release
Demons dissolve
Slayed where they roamed
Small scars remain simply as
Memory

Trickster Tale

Ego is a trickster
It masquerades as wisdom
Shields truth
Promotes illusion

I feel the rising heat as
Ego makes its
grand entrance
taking over with
confusing talk,
loud sounds &
sweeping gestures

It spreads like
wild fire
scalding some while
merely singeing others
some barely notice its
presence but
all are warmed by the
friction it causes

It is deceptive in its
charms
cunning with its
words
skilled in the art of
deception and
creating chaos

Exiting with a deep bow
Ego recedes
for the moment
only to return for its
curtain call

Death & Life

Death reminds us to
Live
Breathe
Appreciate
Love

Death doesn't care
what we have
will never possess
or dream of being

Death is part
of the cycle
of the whole
that is life

Death does not
discriminate
judge
or make demands

Death binds us
in unity
as the one thing
we all share
but experience
alone

Death taps
the depth of
Feeling
Sadness
Solitude
Being

Greet death with a
life-affirming smile
Embrace life with a
sense of mortality

Surfacing

What surfaces from
Way down deep
Bubbles with a knowing that
Has no source

It keeps me present to
Smell the flowers &
Taste the air ~ sometimes
Boiling hot to remind me to
Slow down

My senses pick up what is
In my mind's blind spot
Giving me the courage to
Move on and to
See what is illusory

My occasional choice to
dive into flights of fancy is not
Succumbing to deception or
Trickery or mirage

It is a sacred space where
Imagination thrives and
Informs my deepest truths

Creative vision may be the
deep well that houses the
origin of perception

Perhaps it's all a dream

Forgiveness & Regret

Regret is a cancer
than can be
the undoing
of all the good
that lives
in the moments
between then
and now

Forgiveness
empowers
enlightens
heals

Ownership of action
begins the undoing
slowing the spread
halting metastasis

Confession
creates a
sense of solace
that can put us
in remission

The Show

Stage lights
Make sequins twinkle
Sparkling like magic from a
Distance
The illusory division of proscenium
Lends an extra layer to the
Light

Simple, cheap, ordinary fabrication
Elevated to enchantment simply by
Directing light at the right time
In the right place

Under harsh florescence they
Appear flat and dull yet
A flick of the switch and
A play of guided light can
Change perspective, experience and
Feeling

Oh, that feeling!

Accompanied by story
Scenery and song the
Depth of emotion is stirred
Whirled into a pool of
Memories made and those
Yet dreamed but not lived

The lights go down
Returning the sequins and
The feeling
To darkness
Concealing what was just
Glimpsed of
The possibility of
Living a magical life

Flicker

I lit the candle
The flame flickered
A curious darkness
Squatted on the wick
Swayed with the
Flickering flame
Rooted deep within
The fiery source

The light cast
Shadowy shapes
The walls breathed
Swelling and shrinking
Untethered to reason
All oxygen & attention
Devoted to this dance

Steadiness and flight
Held in equal regard
Ignited imagination
My gaze like a cat's
Darted and landed
Shape-shifted to the
Other side of imagination
Took in the play with
Curiosity and consideration

No room for fear
Only the landscape to
Keep searching for the light

Burn

The brightness burns
Leaving no room for
Imperfection
It shines in every corner
Chasing away fear, envy
Judgment, guilt

Its rays ignite an army of
Self-doubt to scurry
Like mice
Fruitlessly seeking a place
To hide

Vulnerability takes the lead
Encouraging the others to
Shrink beyond detection
Courage shows up
Recognizes the players
And leads them
Directly into the
Spotlight

LIGHT

Through the Fog

peering through
the fog of past
searching for
a clue

the lens of now
resists the quest
what's old
is now what's new

lessons learned need
one more glance
to assure
true understanding

I shake my head
And smile big
And nod
with humor landing

Rising

Open channel
Earth connection
Sinking down
Rising up

Resonance creates
vibrational portal
through which
energy leaps
to the
other side
where mystery
resides and
barriers dissolve
into now

Not closing the doorway
just the concept
of a line
demarking
the space
separating
here
from there

Confined by skin
and bone
yet free
to roam
and discover
beyond the boundary
of body

Breath
unites us

Crumb Trail

Like Hansel
I drop breadcrumbs
when I forge through
parts unknown
though mine
are baked with
ingredients like
potential and
expectations

Still, I wait for them
to lead me home
or at least toward
my life's
purpose

When realization
crashes consciousness
revealing
no crumby trail or
hints to follow

I choose instead to
close my eyes
chase my dreams
and dance to
the beat of
my heart

Taming the Beast

Higher Self
come out to play
ego is talking
and has much to say

I know you're there
I can feel your heat
I must make the choice
not succumb to defeat

I reach out to you now
you rise to that call
what was blocked is now open
now I know I won't fall

Tea

It steeps
I anticipate

Cradling the warm mug between
my palms I lower my head to
better absorb the aroma
Intoxicated, I inhale deeper with
each breath before taking
my first taste

Like love's first kiss
I dissolve under its influence
Surrender to the moment
Fully awake

When the cup is empty, it
remains tepid to the touch
A reminder to remain present, to
breathe deep and embrace the
simple things, finding
joy and meaning with every sip

Blink

waves of shadow
and light
dance behind
my eyelids

offering me
a glimpse
of the infinite
of life's mysteries
of the depth of love

eyes open
the pace of the dance
hastens
to meet the
earthly music

the offering
is now
tactile
specific
familiar

blinking
unites the forces
presenting
a vision of
wholeness
possibility
unity

Bare

bare
they feel and sense
the nuances of
earthly vibrations
connecting us
to the very core
of ourselves, each other
our planet

bare
they gather data
from wet grass
squishy mud
baking boardwalks
soft carpet

mindfully
therapeutically
we articulate heel
baby toe
big toe
offering our steps
to the bigger view
of total well-being

they honor the physical form and
the subtle body
beneath the surface
experiencing life
through the sensations
that arise from below
and spiral upward
linking awareness to
a bigger connection

Look

a glance
a glare
a wink
a stare

the story of the world
can be told by just a look
where words fall short
eyes are our body's book

language can be limiting
actions, misleading
but what you see behind your eyes
is a garden worth seeding

At Play

kids
laughing, giggling, snorting
sharing stories
exercising imagination
figuring it all out

structured play
provides a freedom
which is alive and thriving
within its boundaries
growing confidence
and authentic voice
from the relative safety
of knowing when to say
"when"
or when wildly dancing
over the line
to return later

remove the edifice
erase the lines and
witness

from the chaotic unknown
they create their own
form of structure
which fosters creativity
tapping into unseen gifts
adding layers to the
confidence and voice which
have begun to grow

still, they
laugh, giggle & snort
author their stories
and generously share them
while figuring it all out

Here Now

here now
senses alive
tingling
in every direction
I need only
to pause
and breathe
to feel the
magic

Is this real?

Happiness has always lit my way
Worn carefree like a shawl
 to embrace me during life's ride
 of ups and downs
Who knew there was a sweeter
 space in which to abide
Unexplored terrain leading
 deeper into the forest of
 imagination, dragons and slayers
Where fear outlines shadow, there lives
 a strength of love over which
 no demon can reign victorious
It is there that the heart bursts open and
 true happiness, in its most expansive
 form, is revealed

Bigger Picture

I smile when I hear my sister's
voice come out of my mouth or my
mother's expression pass across
my lips and animate my eyes

I am humbled and grateful for the
open palms and hearts
from guides of many schools of
thought, life and love

It would be misleading to say that
I am a unique expression of something
I unearthed or created
solely with my own hands and
imagination

As a work in progress
I am pieced together
by the resonant tones of my teachers
discovering instead what already
exists that may strike a chord or
ring a bell in my bones

Hear my words and know that
while they come directly from
my heart
they tell a story that includes a much
larger cast

I am shaped by acts of kindness
unusual beauty
truths searching for sound
and all that surrounds me
what I choose to color that shape with
is love

Ripe

Sweet juice dripping down our chins
The taste of summer in every bite
We devour the luscious, pulpy goodness

No care or thought to stopping or slowing
Slurping satisfaction
These are not simple peaches & plums

Their delicious sweetness fills our
Mouths and hearts with equal delight
Until we finish the last one

Laughing at our impulsive act
We fully connect in that very
Ordinary, yet eternal
Moment in our lives

The memory trickles down my mind
like the nectar of yesterday
Wiped gently dry with a grin
A fickle flash in time captured in my
Muscles and bones, rises to the surface
With every ripe, juicy bite

An Open Heart

An open heart
has the capacity
to fall
in love
everyday

Even if the
aperture is
small
it is still
enough

leave something
behind
pick something
up
trade anger
for
joy and
feel the space
where love lives

Take it in
breathe it out
witness
act
feel the love
send it back

Untitled

I can freely give
my heart to one man
but not my beliefs
to one system of thought

I trust the wisdom of
love
it works in every
moment
to clean the filter of my
mind

Spiraling Upward

Toes tingled and
curled
fingers flutter
unfurled

Energy rises from way
deep down
spiraling upward,
caught by the crown
whirling and swirling
around and around

Grounded in love
the source of all things
dizzy with winters
falls, summers and
springs

Activating this life with deeds
thoughts and feelings
sending it out
cracking all the glass ceilings

Moving beyond what
appears to confine
liberating the spirit without
need to define

What bubbles from there is
not short of amazing
it's what makes us all one from
small embers to blazing

Royal Journey

Trust and believe
Question and explore
What you see may be real
Dig deep for much more

Live with curiosity
Love without rules
Choose battles wisely
Keep collecting your tools

Enjoy the adventure
Its ups and its downs
Its joys and its sorrows
These are our crowns

Exodus

The Exodus is now
A mass of individuals
Retreating from confinement
Breath finally released
Liberty no longer restricted
 The invitation extended to
All who seek a larger vision of
The world and the myriad
possibilities it holds
 The risk is premium as are
its rewards
 Take the leap in the direction
of your heart
 Laugh joyfully as you land
 You are free!

Conductor

A chorus of seekers
curious and devoted
magnetize to heart center

Voices raised in unison
singing songs of ancient wisdom
expressing unique timbres
in the pulsating harmonic din of
awakening

The conductors lay down their batons
leaving the choir to bathe
in the unrehearsed melodies
composed by
collective cognizance

Flicker

The fire is a mirror
Flames reaching for the sky
    Spirited by the wind the way
breath animates the body

The force of the blue center
    grounds & kindles the sparks
Providing a seat for their flickers
    While they steadily dwindle to a
bed of hot embers

Reflected back is a hint of
    Human nature
Wild and warm
    Pulsating and alive
Creating a space for the senses
    Crackling coals carry smoky smells
Cutting the cold & deepening breath
    until they fade to dark

Revealing Avalon

The elements of my practice
Echo the elements of Being

Earth, Wind & Fire
Foundation, Breath & Life Force

What can be seen in the world outside
Lives out a potent existence unseen
Within the walls of skin and bone

It is by moving into being alive
That I animate this Avalon inside

Invisible Divide

Distance may lend perspective
but nothing can match the
view from voices raised, hugs shared
eyes held in eternal gaze

The road is long and curvy
Those we meet along the way
are jewels, shiny or rough, they
refract, absorb and shine light
provide refuge in dark times and
loving laughter along the way

I cherish you and you and you for all
you are and continue to become

I love you and the reflection of your heart
What separates cannot divide

Time, miles, experiences
they serve as memorial landmarks and
conversation pieces to honor and
guide us back to each other

Enchanted Crossroads

Running as fast as
I can
On a road
Where the cracks are
Caulked with light
My destination looming

Each footstep
Prodding, leading, guiding
I see a sign but cannot
Read its message

I move my attention to
My steps and not
Where they are taking me

This shift in focus
Slows me down
Sweat pooling on my skin
Breath laboriously looking
For an exit

In the soft stillness that lingers
I find myself standing at
A crossroads
Where magic meets
Imagination

The promise is
A dream
A creative contract to
Keep pushing the
Boundaries of
What is possible

I make the deal

Wishing Well

Hundreds of hearts line up
creating a clear pool of love so deep
its floor exists only in the realm of myth

Differences discarded
tossing shared memories
like pennies
into a wishing well of spirit

Our reflections reveal
something eternal
years dissolve into
moments
moments collapse into
now
now is all there is

Cast your coin!

Untitled

The room holds the same smell from
Nearly forty years ago
I inhale my past deeply
Smile big and let it go

The tribe is built block by block
Joining hearts in joy and sorrow
Looking back to see the work
Forging ahead into tomorrow

It's love that keeps us strong
Holding hands when we feel weak
Hurrying toward a common goal
Dancing slowly cheek to cheek

The village weeps when it feels a loss
And rejoices life each day
We move through this time together
Embraced in a grander sway

Links in the Chain

Somewhere in the middle
Of the road
The journey
My life
To the left, my past
To the right, my future
Planted dead center in my *now*
Ambling forward
Linking the moments together
A sturdy chain is forged
What connects them is a
Range of emotions and memories
But what keeps it linked is
Love

Choices

What if
I chose Boston over NYC?
What if
I loved math more than art?
What if
I were type-A and not XYZ?
What if
I'd practiced yoga from the start?

What would it look like?
How would it smell?
Would I have a different family?
It's a story I cannot tell

Our choices shape our lives
Give them that certain feeling
They plant seeds for what's to come
Set the scene for our believing

I choose to be here now
Reap all that I have sown
Rise tall to each occasion
And embrace it as my own

Fly

magic flew into my life
on the wings of a mythical bird

first she perched on the
branches of my expanding world
then took me along on an
enchanted flight to meet things
as they are
in most extraordinary way

friendship can be alchemical
transforming the mundane
into something wondrous

look closer at your life and
and don't be afraid to fly

Seat of the Teacher

The horizon line is a far as it is wide

Nestled in the Seat of the Teacher,
You have taught me tangible skills
Demonstrated things beyond muscle & bone
Revealed layers of mystery one breath at a time

Perched in the Seat of the Teacher
You shine over shadows
Direct the mind and heart to curious corners
Transmuting fear and the unknown
with revelation, contemplation and insight

From your Seat of the Teacher
You have added countless new seats
Skillfully guiding many eager hands
To hold the sacred space

As you shift your seat, the teacher remains
Radiating a golden light
Embracing the world with a mother's love
Moving through this world with grace
Nourished by the community you built

On the Path

I may not go the farthest
I may stop along the way
I may linger without warning
But I have a lot to say

I may not know the most
I may have a lot to learn
I climb that mountain joyfully
Living into every burn

The heat is in my muscles
It lingers in my mind
It resides within my spirit
It's never hard to find

Shake Up

I need something
To blow my mind
To crack some light
Shake the ground of
habitual complacency
So I may taste the freshness
Lead me from my mind
Landing closer to the source

Words

The words they
Write themselves
Write themselves
Write themselves
Fully formed capsules of
Meaning
Nuance
Purpose
Until
Like drops of water on a
Scalding surface
Scalding surface
Scalding surface
They sizzle
Then evaporate
Returning to the ether
Of imagination

The Gift of Now

Today is a gift
Will you open it or
Leave it unwrapped?

If you open it
Will you care for its contents
Or drop it and walk away?

Is your path littered with the possibility of
Unopened boxes?
Or is it strewn with their remnants?

Not every package needs
To be opened
Nor is every pretty present
Worth examining

The daily opening is an
Internal endowment
That we get to glimpse
Bit by bit
Over a lifetime

Get Lost

I don't mind being lost
Staggering through strange terrain
Dancing with unknown shapes
Being present with a light step
Courage makes its mark on my
Quickly beating heart
Reminding me I am alive
That is enough for now

Whimsy

A traveling minstrel
with the soul of a bard
rode right through our hearts
and skipped through the yard

His spirit on high
and his heart on his sleeve
he got us all dancing
and with no sound took his leave

Exploration

nestling purposefully into the space
between who i am & who i was
there's space to be free & explore
the mysteries of self just because

Rays of Light

the sun is shining
the kids are smiling
intentions of gratitude
can be quite beguiling

Living in Light

humble and curious
anchored in truth
compassionate heart
mystery's sleuth

approach yourself softly
with humor and love
the light's been ignited
from within and above

Open Window

one day a door closes on a dream
you watch it drift as if down a stream
the window you heard would open, lifts
along with the breeze, in flies new gifts

Fan the Flames

Be the breath
Stoke the fire
Transformation
Will transpire

Seeker

treading the path
searching and seeking
finding and losing
observing and peeking

fluidly moving
as student and teacher
learning and growing
without help from a preacher

heart open wide
arms poised for embrace
lovingly curious
through time and through space

Ordinary

adventures of ordinary proportions
present themselves each day
as thrilling as anything exotic
and nourishing in every way

The Urgency of Now

The urgency of now
lingers ever in our lives
Infusing every moment
with an element of surprise

Bearing witness to one's life
may seem mundane indeed
But asking for much more at once
may be misconstrued as greed

Watching fluffy clouds float by
morphing characters into plot
Leaves me feeling rather small
and oh so grateful for my lot

Wonder

a fleeting moment of wonder
releases an eternity of awe
curiosity takes its rightful place
playful, joyous, thoughtful, raw

Magic of the Moment

a piece of music makes me smile
an old friend calls and warms my heart
i settle in and take a breath
each new moment's a work of art

Community

alone behind
the red-tinged
darkness
of closed eyes
i experience
this life
from the
inside

awake but alone
i am
surrounded
by the
collective energy
of the people
who
populate my life

by choice
or by
circumstance
i am not alone
but part
of something
bigger than
my solitary
existence

nourished by
breath
imagination
creativity
and love
of the other
solitary beings
we create
community

punctuated by
moments of
pure joy
inconsolable sadness
laughter
and tears
comedy
and tragedy

we help
each other
shoulder
life's burdens

we learn
we grow
we breathe
we live

together

Horizon Lines

The urban skyline
silhouettes the scope
of what is possible

The natural vistas
show a vision of beauty
beyond our making

In concert
they illuminate
the inner landscape
of dreams

String of Pearls

The light from the flame reveals a shadow dance
My eyes follow the blinking shapes
In constant motion, they tell a story
Like a string of bulbs creating a mood
They are moments strung together
Telling a temporal tale of twos
Dualities flash
Dark & bright
Heavy & light

Family Diagnosis

My parents have cancer
Their lives unhinged yet they
Remain tethered to the world
Using the tools they've cultivated over
A lifetime
Humor
Connection
Love

Every new day offers the
Opportunity
To practice
Firing the malleable clay of ideals
In the scorching fire of the
Unknown
They dive in
Blistering heat tests
Faith
Fear
Foundation

What emerges from the flames is
Solid yet porous
Steady yet shaky
Beautiful and flawed
Leaving the new "normal"
Unglazed
At least for now
We rejoice in the
Purity of each breath and the
Infinite possibilities

Laughter finds the fissures
Infusing them with something
Stronger than
Chemo and scalpels
Leaving medicinal
Odors and protocols to
Burn away into
Cheerful, colorful landscapes
Of hope and
Wonder

Their open hearts and
Generous souls
Open the doors and windows
Daily to rising suns
The light from which
Illuminates the path
Step by step
Without a glimpse beyond tomorrow

So, today, we laugh
Finding ways to joke and tease
In the rays of sunshine that
Live between the dark shadows
Choreographing a joyous dance
Inviting all to move to the beat
To lose ourselves in the sway

There is nothing
Unresolved
In what passes between us
For that I am
Grateful

The Eyes Have It

Mom's eyes
Dark brown
Expressive
Divine pools of love
Mirroring
Prism reflections

Dad's beautiful blue eyes
Obscured by
Thick, cloudy
Lenses
Come clear with
Age
Diving through the
Deep end of my
Soul

Mine show hazel
More brown than green but
Always true, they
Hold their gaze in mine and
Connect to the bright
Source that allows
Pure vision

WILD FLOWERS ~
NATURE'S WINDOW

Isolation

Isolation is an illusion
Connection is key

I feel the earth tremble
in its eternal effort to keep spinning
Gasp with lungs burning
as the air chokes
Starve with a full belly of GMOs
Dissolve into the oceans
as they die away
releasing us from our
link to each other
and Earth Mother

Is this it?
When did we lose our way?

I circle back like a hawk
observing its prey
Determined to
infuse, bemuse and swoop in
devouring only what I need
honoring the elements
reconnecting the dots
perhaps it's not too late

Stewards of Our Planet

Gazing out from way up high
the view is astounding
a mountain of salt
where oceans once
ebbed and flowed

Impressions and depressions
punctuate a barren landscape
once thriving and
vibrating with life
pulsations now eerie and still

What remains is
beyond memory
a whisper of life
flickering like a
flame in the wind
its blue center now
dull and cool
no longer scorching
animated or vital

Love, riding the
directionless breeze to
places unknown
sowing its life-affirming seed
lands lightly, taking root
In this new soil
nurturing what is to come

Raindrops

Drop by drop the rain falls
Forming diamonds on
Branches
Nourishing sleeping
Seedlings
Quenching a deep, abiding
Thirst

Lightly, they patter on
Earthly structures
Sing songs of
Renewal
Set the beat for life's
Rhythm

The wind swells
Empowering the drops with
power to destroy

Can we see one raindrop
In the storm?

Eyes open to the sky
Water cascading down
Smooth surfaces
Creating
Waterfall of life
We are all raindrops

Forecast

Rather than moan
about the volume
of snow that has dropped
and the forecast of
even more snow to fall,
I choose to
joyfully embrace it,
knowing
at least for now
this moment in
time
I am here
to feel it
to witness its
majestic beauty

If I am
inconvenienced
or forced to
improvise my
well-laid plans
to accommodate something
as untamed and
purposeful
as mother nature
I will rejoice
and celebrate that
I am here
to navigate such
magical terrain

Awaiting Spring

bare winter limbs
foreground to a
bright blue sky
whisper hints of
what's to come

expressive
like hands
they tell the story
of hardships
overcome
and joys unfolding

dissolving
inevitably
into the ever-changing
season of all things

rooted to the
earth
and connected
to the sentient
world
we move
slowly

riding the
steady breeze of
our collective breath
into the renaissance
of an awaiting spring

Impermanence

feeling the feeling
letting it go
joy meets grief
spring melts snow

Raindrops Calling

every raindrop
sounds a call
pounding storm or
light drizzle

allow its force to
wake us up
else in sunshine's light
we fizzle

Ducks

the ducks are back
it must be Spring
they foretell the season
beyond the reason
of mere dates on the calendar

without fail
they tell the tale
of Mother Nature's
wisdom
by moving from that
place inside
without striving
or agenda
just being
who they are

to watch them
walk
side by side
finding their stride
exploring their world
is a joy and a
reminder to
listen closely to what is
not spoken

Witness

imagine such stories
as the trees, mountains
rivers and oceans
could tell

they are witnesses
to the slow moving
pace of evolution
impermanence is
the constant in every tale

as humans and animals
pass through
marking lifetimes
in moments
the natural world
moves in seasons
slowly drawing a picture that
will never be completed

Flutter

Inspiration flutters
like leaves flapping in the breeze
some remain tethered to their branches
while others blow away
or drift slowly to the ground

A cyclone of petals
whirling around and around
wildly
while the wind, unseen, but
felt and heard,
provides a structure for the
chaos to find order

The wind slows down
dissolving the walls containing the petals
allowing them the freedom to fall
journeying downward
making contact with the earth

They dance,
These earthly elements
of nature
to the music of the Universe
weaving under and over each other
creating a cloth under which we
all take cover

There's a knowing, deep inside,
a wisdom of change and movement
Impermanence

Those still holding on to
branches and stems
look on
Inspired as they
they flutter

Dew Drops

the dew glistens on each
blade of grass
reflecting the earth's wisdom
from beauty to survival

a single drop of dew
holds in its tiny pool
a world of simplicity
and asks nothing of the world
but to serve its function

stepping into my day
I walk across the grass
and inhale the first breaths of Spring
unaware of the chaos
my footsteps inflict upon this
daily natural happening

without emotion or reprimand
the destruction of these
intentionally temporal dewdrops
yields to the silence and stillness
necessary to the moments before
creation

Mother Nature's cogs
are turning to the
rhythm of life
the sun dries the morning's moisture
guiding the day to its next
phase

all is as it should be

Autumn Slays Me!

the play of light
through the trees
reflects a clarity
born from an
eternity
of change
from one season
to the next

vibrant colors
ride on sunbeams
flash a glimpse
of their brief purpose
and everlasting heart-print
on this earth
and to my moment
as witness

the satisfying crunch
underfoot
makes a sound that
echoes back
to the innocence & curiosity
of childhood
revealing the truth that
time
is not
fixed

Crunch

Brisk
Blue
Sky
cradles the leaves
as they are released
from their perches and
float down to
that space where
earth
meets the horizon

Crunching
crispness
collides with
clear, rich
colors,
creating
colluding
conspiring
bringing autumn
to life

Echoing the subtle
vibrations
rippling on the
breeze
the ground receives
these seasonal
gifts of
dissolution
determined and

defiant
moving into the
next phase
into the
stillness
before the
quiet cover of
winter is
created

We enter this
moment
like all moments
before this one
resting in its
inevitable now-ness
calm or agitated
it will soon pass
and turn into
something else
something new
inviting us in
to learn
to love
to be
in the sharp
potent
vision of now
as the reverie
fades
into a
new dream

Melting into Spring

tiny buds
are forming
where ice crystals
once defined
the shape of things,
brushing color
onto the
landscape of
whites and grays

awakening
from the depths
of the earth, where
warmth
waited patiently
for the blustery
winds of winter
to subside
it arises

the ducks
reliably return
to the pond,
floating on its
winter-chilled
glassy surface,
foretelling the
season of
rebirth

the flow
of change
sweeps me into
its strong
embrace

I bow to its
benevolent force
and surrender
completely
to its wisdom

Nestled in Nature

Dawn's daily footprint
Is a soft reminder to wake up
Its light gradually fills the horizon
As we slowly wipe the sleep from our eyes
April showers hydrate the earth as
Rain drops gently from an infinite **Sky**
Clues and messages for how to thrive are
Nestled in nature's nooks
Pause, notice and follow
Nature's trail

Birthing Spring

Baby buds appear on thin branches
spots of color spread
uncovering secret centers of life
gradually blossoming to
full expression

Thrashing winds draw the
branches into a wild dance
further opening to the magic of
Spring's Renaissance

Earth's whipping breath
unseen but for the movement it
inspires in the space between things
expands the circle
excludes nothing
unites us all

Personal Spring

Resurrect your hopes and dreams
Lay fear and doubt to rest
The soil's fertile, seedlings root
It's Mother Nature at her best

Spring is here with signs of life
Freedom and rebirth for all
Second chances blossom everywhere
Quiet down to hear the call

Rise up grounded to meet yourself
Wherever it is you are
Location shifts with every breath
From your heart you're never far

Earth Dance

My soles vibrate with Earth underfoot
feeling the rumblings of new life surging
through the roots of my arches and
the trunk of my spine, I am one with her

Her breath weaves through the leaves of my hair
massages my mind and tingles my senses
delivering messages from great distances and faraway
times

Her heart-song is a never-ending chorus of
forward motion melodies sung by her children
four legs or two we move, trancelike, to the
pulsating rhythms of her ancient, yet relevant wisdom

Take off your shoes and feel this connection
Let's dance!

Joy of Winter

I love Winter
Trees bare to the bones
Nature's truth unveiled
Space galore
But no room to hide

The wind
Swoons and croons
Feeling its way
Inviting the naked limbs
To join
Its feral dance

Gazing upward
I succumb
Shedding the layers
Of self
Revealing my own nature
No escape
Only one choice
Join the jig

Perseverance & Possibility

I rise slightly to behold the horizon
Its distant line both
delineates and joins
heaven and earth
honoring our individuality while
revealing the oneness
of all things

I bow back to the earth
Touching that which grounds me in
Body, mind, heart and spirit
Rooted to the Mother, I lift
Heart and hands to the sky
My earthly nature ascends
To meet the Divine

Drawing my hands to my source
The rhythmic beating a reminder
of life's interconnected pulsations

I lift my toes and
Close my eyes
To better feel the subtlety of flow
Earth meets Sky
The mountain will be moved

Joyous Breath

the breeze washes over me
revealing its invisible nature by
tingling the hairs on my arms and neck
animating the blades of grass around my bare feet

the easy flow of air slowly builds to gusts of wind
inviting the trees to dance and sway and the flags
to flap and unfurl to express their wilder nature

my breath picks up the flow
vitality pulsating on my inhalation
surrender settling with my exhalation

clear to the eye, its texture and taste
expose its presence
as it courses through the shell
of my body

every movement originating from
the cradle of my breath
I laugh and my breath becomes a
vehicle for joy

Alive

Waking up to the sound of
Raindrops outside
Open windows on a crisp
Autumn morning
Slowly unfolding body
Unwrapping mind
Inhaling fresh promises
Of another day to
Be alive

Ode to Winter

winter will enter
its cold air and soft snow
an enchantment its own
and then it will go

spring will return
re-infusing our senses
with hope and good cheer
looking through rose-colored lenses

and then when we blink
it's summer once more
fun sunny days
who could ask for more

each season is wondrous
unique in its glory
thank goodness this isn't
the end of that story

Our Story

What if the sky whispered its secrets to you?
The sky
Eternal witness
Quietly whispers its millennia-old memories
Scattering secrets like seeds
Pollinating stories that turn to legends
Origin myths buried deep beneath the surface
Rise to inspire new tales to be told and retold

What if the earth answered back?
Fertile and arid, both
Sharing its ever-changing landscape of perception
Marred & celebrated by the countless footsteps that
Stomp her face through generations of life
Her heroes, too many to count, too few to mention
Give voice and movement to those tales

Creatures of sea, air and land all play their parts
Creating and destroying
Living and hibernating
Swimming, flying, running & jumping
Eating, drinking
Laughing and loving

The clouds give cover to a low horizon
Patches of blue peek through the cottony blanket
Winking to wake us up
Beckoning for a listening ear
To come close enough to
Hear Her story

Nature's Grace

Enchantment surround us ~ the
misty moments marinate in
nature's grace
providing glimpses of grandeur
Air turns to drops of water, landing on
blades of grass
roof & tree tops
bare skin

Absorbed into the life-force of the
tangible world, the unseen
vapor enhances the vigor of our
commitment to be present ~
It communicates in a primal way as a
reminder to
look up
walk firmly
love more

Spring's infancy reveals budding bits of
Untold truths ~ Winter's white sky will
Soon turn to blue
bewitching us as we witness
the eternal in moments

Flow

Wild & ordered
Chaotic & calm
Nature reflects our
Intrinsic character
Echoes our needs & desires
It shows us how be…
It flows & ripples with
Our thoughts & actions
It breathes us
Sustains us
Loves us

Uncertainty

I know I'm meant to write about a particular topic or title
I think it has something to do with grass and a river but
My mind keeps wandering, taking me to other landscapes
Rolling hills, green and deep ravines
Mountains, ice caps and slopes of snow
Desert sand burns my feet, leading me to
Unknown destinations
Sun rays illuminate the way, darkening peripheral distractions
Revealing only what matters
Cool grass beneath my soles send shivers up my spine
Rippling like the rapids on the river; and so I make
Full circle

Nature Poetic

Nature crafts poetry
Where phrases fail
And tells the stories
Our hearts write

It soothes the rough edges
When sadness creeps in
Reveals unseen forces as
They work tirelessly
On our behalf and the
Unspoken words that lay
Dormant under our tongues

When the verbal and written
Declarations cease, we are left with
Color, line, shape and texture
Scent, taste and imagination

The music of the wind
Carries the genius of these songs
Far and wide
They grow and loom
large around us while
The earth keeps turning

Ray of Hope

It's raining so hard
The drops band together to create a barrier
that prohibits movement,
numbs all my senses and leaves me disoriented

I am deafened by the massive chorus of sound and
paralyzed by the torrential force of this squall
Panic stands sentry on the surface of my mind
allowing entrance in the space between my breaths

Like a bellows, I force more air into my lungs
Expanding the possibility of more oxygen
And find a brief sense of calm
where agitation once abided

Blinking my eyes to clear my vision
I gaze out to see a break in the rain
The downpour is now a drizzle and the moisture
beads on the laughing leaves as a gentle
breeze breathes new life and sight where
just a moment before was a blinding barrage of bedlam

In the silence that follows a ray is revealed and
I see a faint hint of hope beyond my window
In the sky of dreams is an arc
of thick pastel lines now fading into the infinite blue

At once, fierce and foreboding
Without warning, serene and still
I take solace in the impermanence and
message of being in the moment
What arrived as worry has subsided into
unshakable surrender

Call of the Wild

I hear a piece of beautiful music
See an extraordinary performance
Taste a perfectly prepared bite and
Feel the prana ripple across my chest

This promise of life-force energy
Surging through the layers of my being
Is a pact between myself and the world
To absorb what is offered with simple sincerity

I look out of myself and witness nature's wonder
The song of the birds
The dance of the deer
The sweet honeysuckle in full bloom

I am no less awed by these ordinary occurrences
My heart blossoms with the fullness of it all
As my pulse undulates effortlessly to its rhythm
Answering the call of the wild

Ninja

she moves with the grace and
ferocity of a tigress
measured and wild
she takes what she needs and
leaves the rest
nuzzling nature
without attachment
her strength lies in her
quiet confidence and
liquid humor that
rides her breath in ripples of
laughter and song
a ray of sunshine captures her
rare beauty
shining in its hazy light
all is clear

Our senses grasp what our minds discard

About the Author

Born in 1968, Sherry carries the free-spirited aspect of that decade in her heart.

Family, friends, yoga, meditation, writing, public speaking and connecting with the diversity of humankind are the essential elements that make Sherry tick.

Inspired by her years in Manhattan and those that followed in Bucks County, PA, Sherry is on a lifetime journey to find her voice and share what she discovers with others.

Influenced early on by theatre and music, Sherry received a degree in Acting from NYU's Tisch School of the Arts and found herself dancing regularly in the great party that was the Grateful Dead. She worked many jobs including a two-year tenure at Wetlands Preserve, a rock and roll environmentally aware night club in NYC, which she maintains was a magical time. Earning her Masters in Media Studies from the New School for Social Research while building her real-life skills on the job, Sherry's curiosity kept moving her forward. She met many remarkable people along her way and while acting never manifested as her career (by choice), Sherry eventually found her true voice as a teacher of the things she loves most.

It was the yoga teacher training program at the Prancing Peacock, that was meant to simply deepen her practice, that took her by surprise and shook up her world. Her husband, Brian, implored her to teach at least one class. Well, that one class turned into two, three, four and before she knew it, Sherry had found a new career. It wasn't so much teaching the poses that kept leading her down this path, but the connections they stirred and the relationships they grew.

Sherry feels that yoga and poetry are keystones to communicating the beauty and possibility that life holds for us all. They are vehicles for uniting and reminding us that we are not separate from each other or our world. It is in the profound moments between sound and silence, the written and spoken word, pain and pleasure, love and fear, hope and dreams that we truly join together. Sherry's greatest wish is to contribute to expanding awareness and love that allows us to live from our best selves and highest vibration.

Sherry is a wife, mother of three, yoga teacher at the ERYT200, RYT500 level, Reiki Master and published author. She continues to practice, teach and train in various aspects of yoga, as well as, write about her experiences and observations in her Blog, **_Drop & Give Me Yoga!_** when time permits.

Sherry has had two poems published in Volume I of _The Poetry of Yoga_ (HawaH), several articles published in local papers and online publications and continues to seek out venues for her work. Sherry put out her first collection of poems, through Balboa Press in 2015 entitled, _Love's Wild Journey ~ Poems from an Untamed Heart._

Made in the USA
Middletown, DE
24 May 2019